Trace and write **A**.   **A** is for **alligator** and **anchor**.

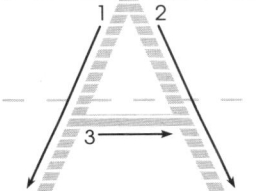

Trace and write **a**.

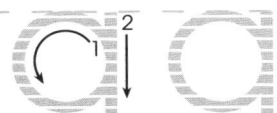

Write **a** to begin the words. Color the pictures.

_____pple   _____nt

Bb

Trace and write **B**.

B is for **boat** and **bear**.

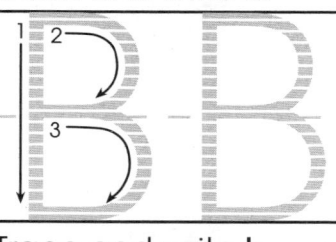

Trace and write **b**.

Write **b** to begin the words. Color the pictures.

_____ug   _____utterfly

2

Trace and write **C**. C is for **cake** and **cow**.

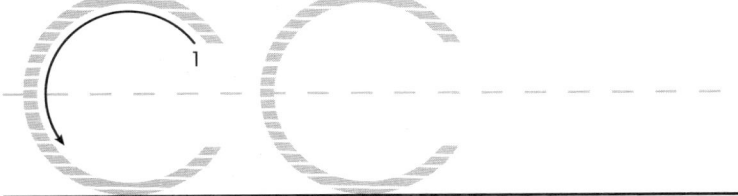

Trace and write **c**.

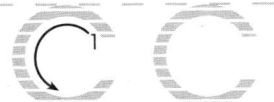

Write **c** to begin the words. Color the pictures.

_____at   _____ar

3

Dd

Trace and write **D**.　　　**D** is for **drum** and **doghouse**.

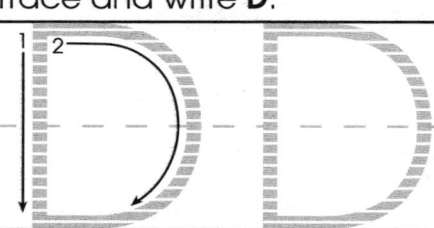

Trace and write **d**.

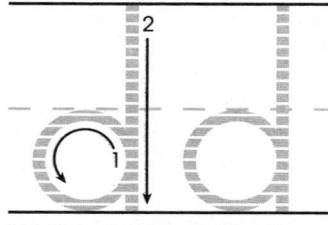

Write **d** to begin the words. Color the pictures.

_____og　　　　_____oll

4

Draw lines from the pictures to the letters that begin their names. Circle the picture that does not belong.

Help the apple farmer pick apples.
Draw lines from the uppercase letters
to the matching lowercase letters.

B

A

C

D

d

c

b

a

A B C D

Find and circle the hidden pictures. Color the scene.

ant   apple   bone   ball   corn   car   duck   drum

Ee

 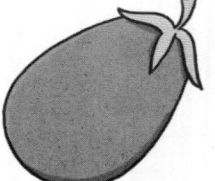

Trace and write **E**.

E is for **envelope** and **eggplant**.

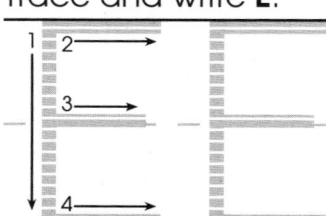

Trace and write **e**.

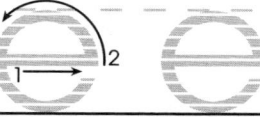

Write **e** to begin the words. Color the pictures.

_____lephant _____gg

Ff

  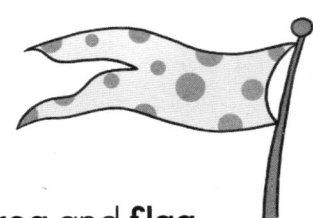

Trace and write **F**.

F is for **frog** and **flag**.

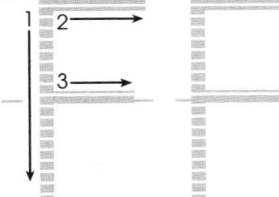

Trace and write **f**.

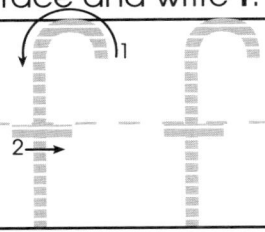

Write **f** to begin the words. Color the pictures.

_____lower _____ish

Gg

Trace and write **G**.

G is for **girl** and **goose**.

Trace and write **g**.

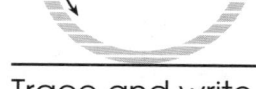

Write **g** to begin the words. Color the pictures.

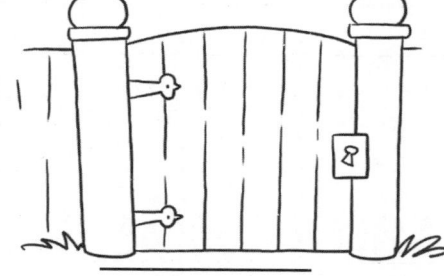

_____ift

_____ate

Hh

Trace and write **H**.   **H** is for **hamburger** and **hen**.

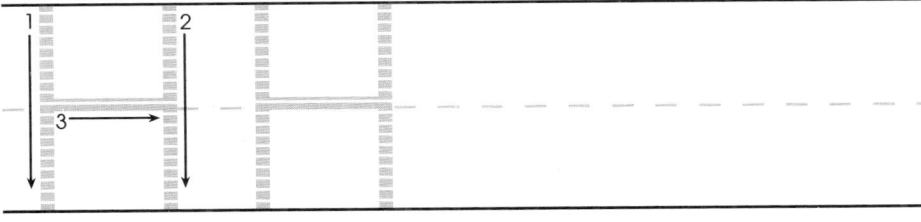

Trace and write **h**.

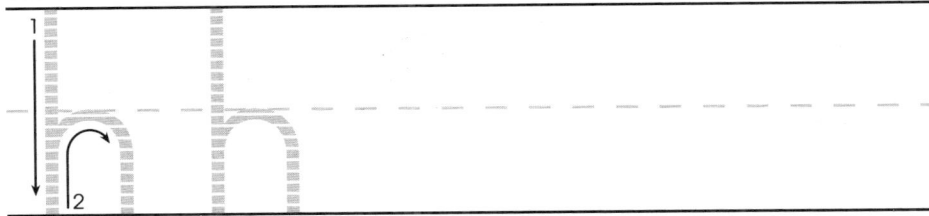

Write **h** to begin the words. Color the pictures.

_____eart   _____at

Draw lines from the pictures to the letters that begin their names. Circle the picture that does not belong.

e

f

g

h

Help the rockets get to the correct planets.
Draw lines from the uppercase letters
to the matching lowercase letters.

g

e

h

f

F

H

G

E

E F G H

Find and circle the hidden pictures. Color the scene.

egg   eagle   fire   fish   gift   guitar   hat   hook

I i

 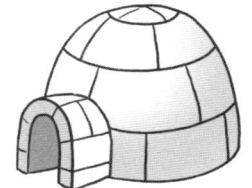 

Trace and write **I**.

I is for **igloo** and **iguana**.

Trace and write **i**.

Write **i** to begin the words. Color the pictures.

_____nsect   _____nk

Jj

Trace and write **J**.

J is for **jump rope** and **jeep**.

J J

Trace and write **j**.

j j

Write **j** to begin the words. Color the pictures.

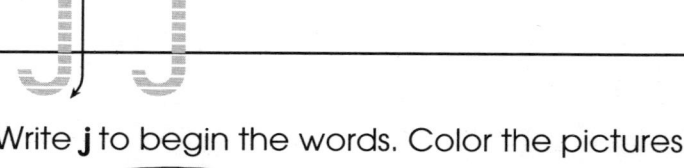

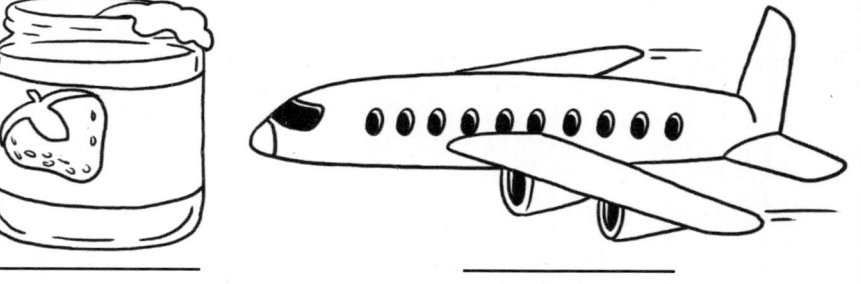

_____elly   _____et

16

Kk

Trace and write **K**.   **K** is for **kitten** and **key**.

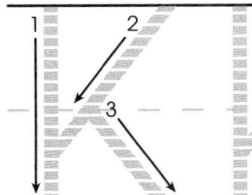

Trace and write **k**.

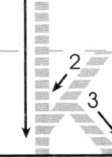

Write **k** to begin the words. Color the pictures.

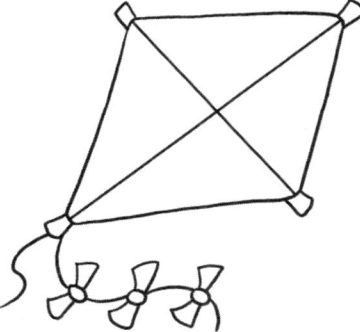

_____oala   _____ite

Ll

Trace and write **L**.

L is for **lion** and **lemon**.

1↓   2→⟶ L

Trace and write **I**.

1↓

Write **l** to begin the words. Color the pictures.

_____ock   _____eaf

Draw lines from the pictures to the letters that begin their names. Circle the picture that does not belong.

Help the race cars cross the finish line.
Draw lines from the uppercase letters
to the matching lowercase letters.

I J K L

Find and circle the hidden pictures. Color the scene.

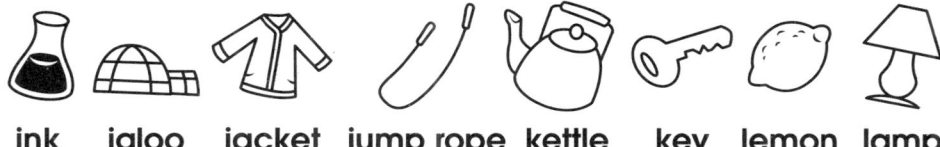

ink   igloo   jacket   jump rope   kettle   key   lemon   lamp

Mm

 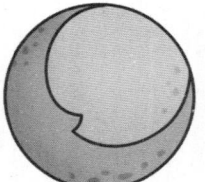

Trace and write **M**.

M is for **mouse** and **moon**.

Trace and write **m**.

Write **m** to begin the words. Color the pictures.

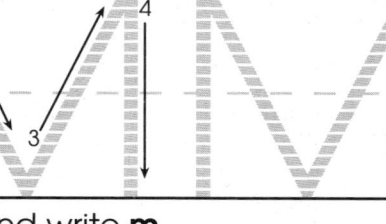 

_____onkey _____itten

Nn

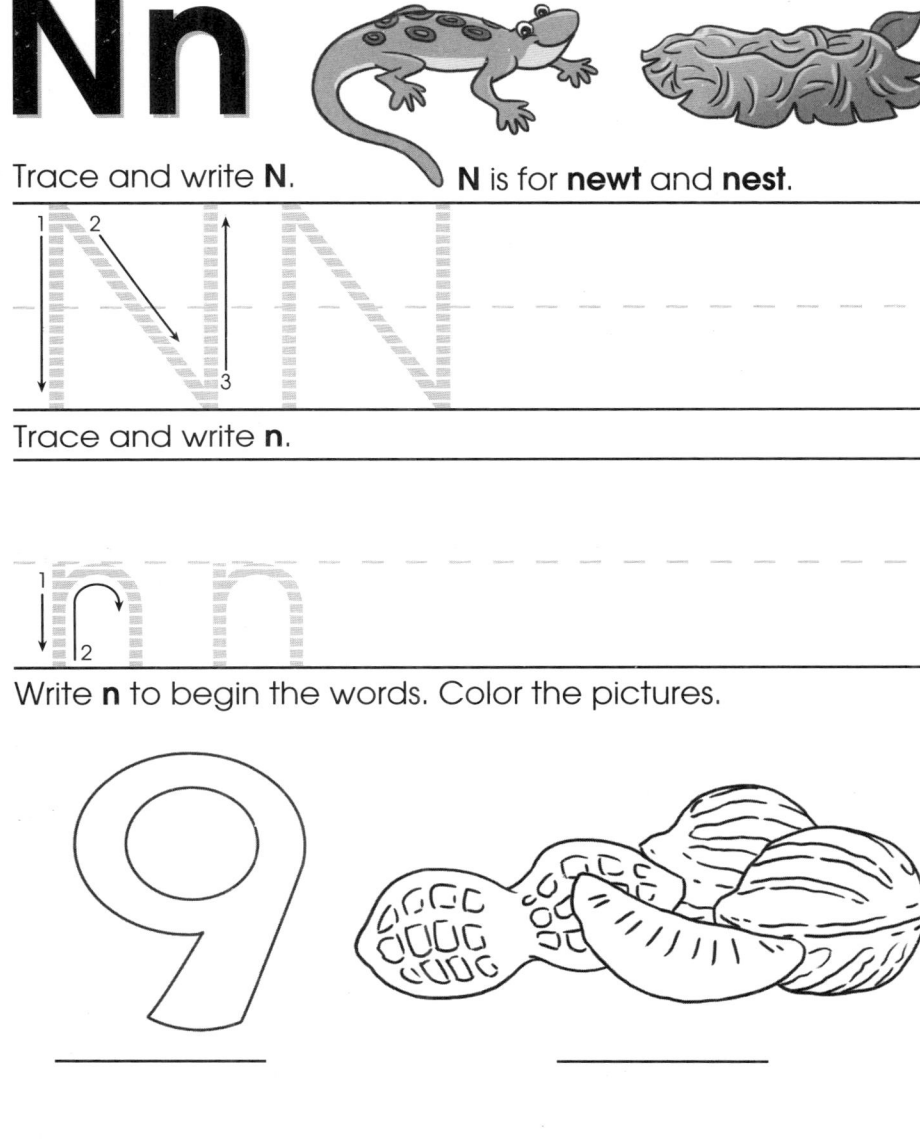

Trace and write **N**.

N is for **newt** and **nest**.

Trace and write **n**.

Write **n** to begin the words. Color the pictures.

_____ine

_____uts

 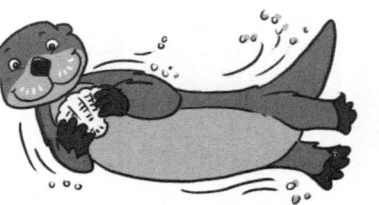 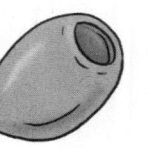

Trace and write **O**.   **O** is for **otter** and **olive**.

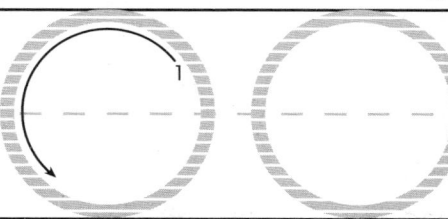

Trace and write **o**.

Write **o** to begin the words. Color the pictures.

_____ctopus _____wl

Pp

Trace and write **P**.

P is for **pumpkin** and **penguin**.

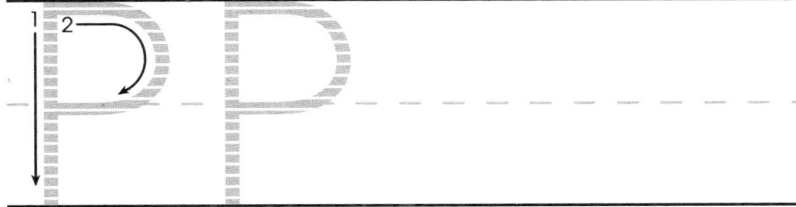

Trace and write **p**.

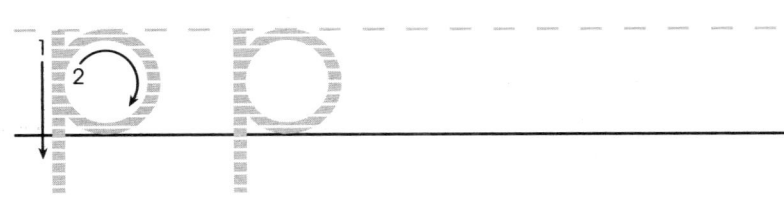

Write **p** to begin the words. Color the pictures.

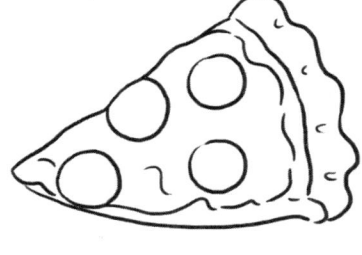 

_____izza   _____ig

Draw lines from the pictures to the letters that begin their names. Circle the picture that does not belong.

Help fill the ice cream cones at the fair.
Draw lines from the uppercase letters
to the matching lowercase letters.

Today's flavors:
Nutty Buddy
Peppermint
Moose Tracks
Orange Dream

MNOP

Find and circle the hidden pictures. Color the scene.

moon   mug   nest   necklace   olive   oven   pillow   pencil

Qq

Trace and write **Q**.

Q is for **quail** and **quarter**.

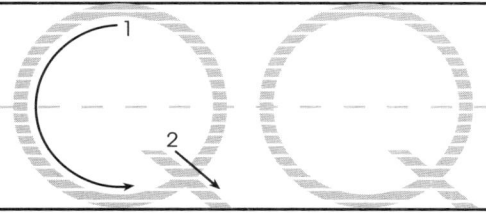

Trace and write **q**.

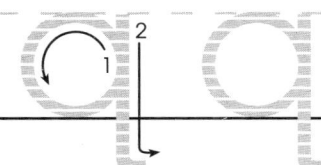

Write **q** to begin the words. Color the pictures.

_____   _____

_____uilt   _____ueen

Rr

Trace and write **R**.

R is for **rabbit** and **ring**.

Trace and write **r**.

Write **r** to begin the words. Color the pictures.

_____ug

_____ocket

Ss

Trace and write **S**.

S is for **sun** and **sailboat**.

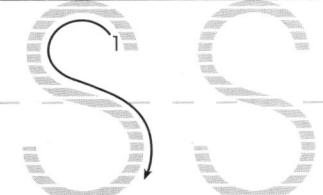

Trace and write **s**.

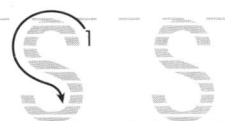

Write **s** to begin the words. Color the pictures.

_____tar   _____nail

Tt

Trace and write **T**.

T is for **turtle** and **turkey**.

Trace and write **t**.

Write **t** to begin the words. Color the pictures.

_____ruck   _____op

Draw lines from the pictures to the letters that begin their names. Circle the picture that does not belong.

Help fly the kites.
Draw lines from the uppercase letters
to the matching lowercase letters.

Q R S T

Find and circle the hidden pictures. Color the scene.

quarter   quail   ring   rocket   sock   stamp   trophy   tie

Uu

Trace and write **U**.

U is for **underwear** and **up**.

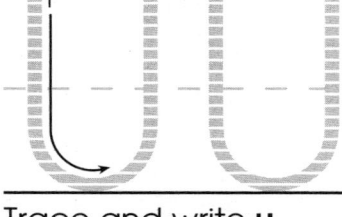

Trace and write **u**.

Write **u** to begin the words. Color the pictures.

_____mpire _____mbrella

36

V v

Trace and write **V**.   **V** is for **vase** and **vegetables**.

1 2

Trace and write **v**.

1 2

Write **v** to begin the words. Color the pictures.

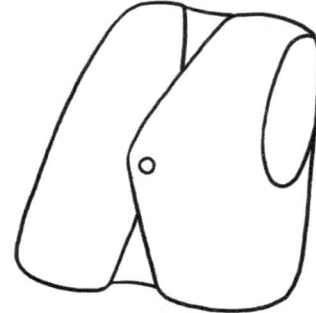

_____an   _____est

W w

Trace and write **W**.

W is for **web** and **watermelon**.

Trace and write **w**.

Write **w** to begin the words. Color the pictures.

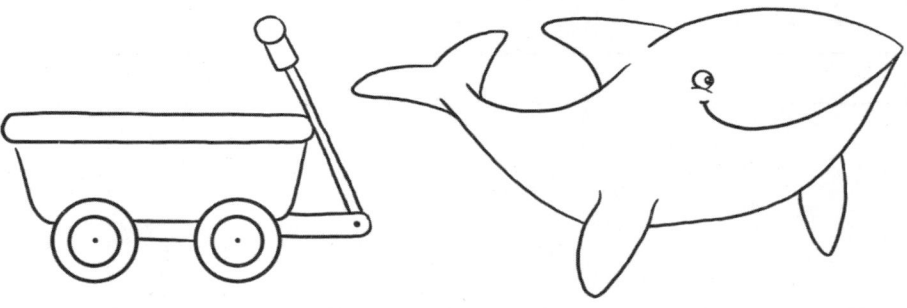

_____ _____

_____agon _____hale

Trace and write **X**.

X is for **x-ray**.

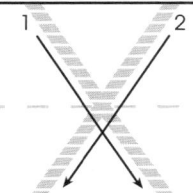

Trace and write **x**.

Write **x** to end the words. Color the pictures.

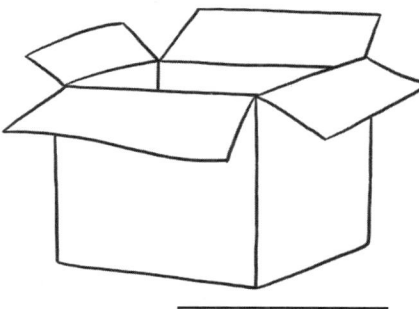

fo _____

bo _____

Draw lines from the pictures to the letters that begin their names. Circle the picture that does not belong.

Help the frogs get to the correct lily pads.
Draw lines from the uppercase letters
to the matching lowercase letters.

Yy

Trace and write **Y**.

Y is for **yarn** and **yams**.

Trace and write **y**.

Write **y** to begin the words. Color the pictures.

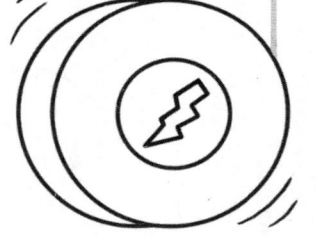

_____ellow _____o-yo

42

Zz

Trace and write **Z**.   **Z** is for **zebra** and **zipper**.

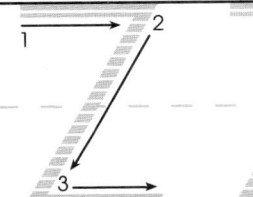

Trace and write **z**.

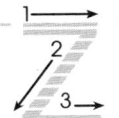

Write **z** to begin the words. Color the pictures.

_____oo   _____ero

U V W X Y Z

Find and circle the hidden pictures. Color the scene.

up vase van whale watch x-ray yarn zipper

Help the ant get to the picnic. Follow the path from **A** to **Z**.

A B C D E F G H I J K L M N O P Q R S T U V W X Y Z

Help the pirate get to the treasure. Follow the path from **a** to **z**.

a b c d e f g h i j k l m n o p q r s t u v w x y z

Connect the dots from **A** to **Z**. Color the picture.

A B C D E F G H I J K L M N O P Q R S T U V W X Y Z

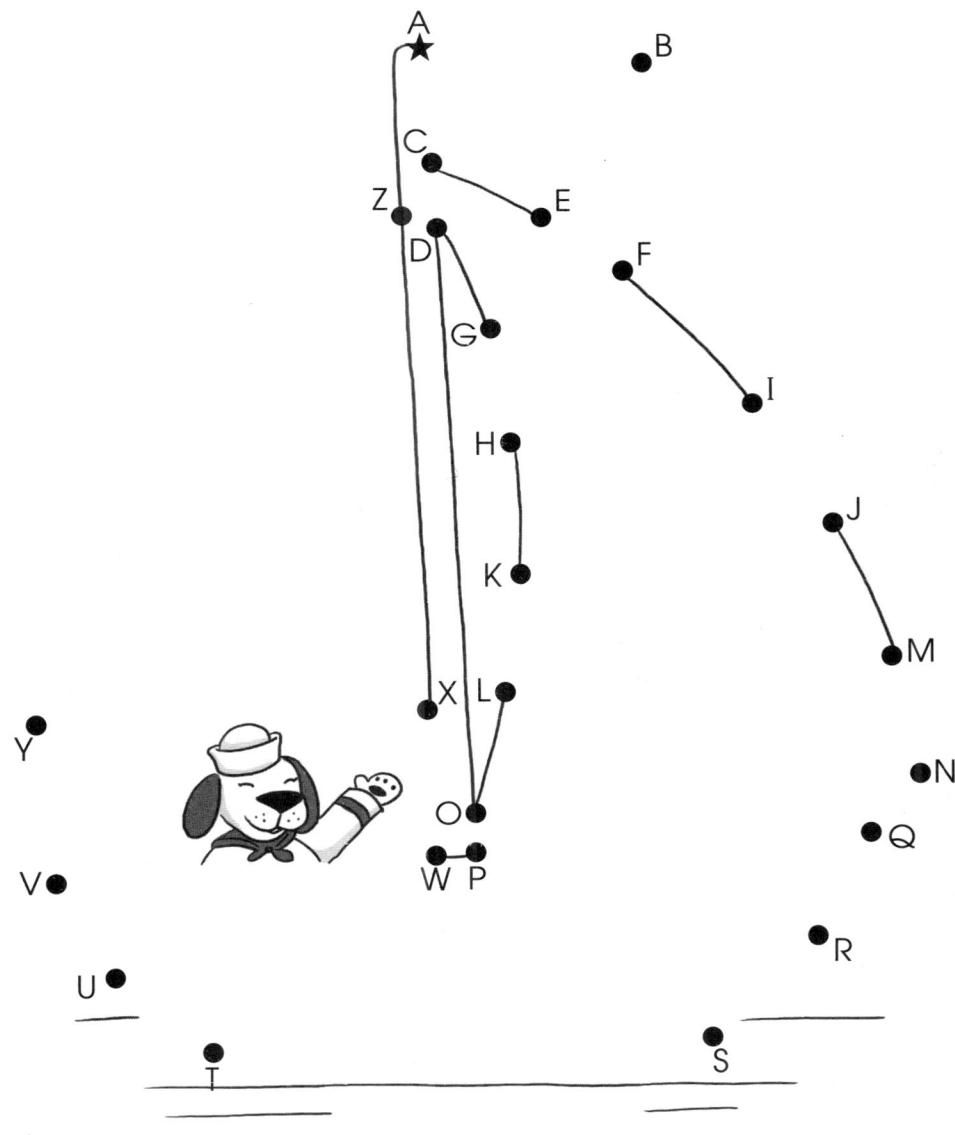

Connect the dots from **a** to **z**. Color the picture.

a b c d e f g h i j k l m n o p q r s t u v w x y z